GHOSTS AND HAUNTED PLACES

INVESTIGATING HISTORY'S MYSTERIES

Louise Spilsbury

Published in 2024 by **Cheriton Children's Books**
1 Bank Drive West, Shrewsbury, Shropshire, SY3 9DJ, UK

First Edition

Author: Louise Spilsbury
Designer: Jessica Moon
Editor: Jennifer Sanderson
Proofreader: Katie Dicker

Picture credits: Cover: Shutterstock/Patrick Foto (fg), Shutterstock/mRGB (bg). Inside: p1: Shutterstock/Dominionart, p4: Shutterstock/Raggedstone, p5: Shutterstock/Tom Tom, p6: Shutterstock/Kiselev Andrey Valerevich, p7: Shutterstock/Dan Kosmayer, p8: Shutterstock/Lario Tus, p9: Shutterstock/Valery Sidelnykov, p10: Wikimedia Commons/ William H Mumler, p11: Shutterstock/Andreiuc88, p12: Shutterstock/Lia Koltyrina, p13: Shutterstock/Marcin Mierzejewski, p14: Shutterstock/Gwoeii, p15: Shutterstock/ Roman Nerud, p16: Wikimedia Commons, p17b: Shutterstock/Sandra Cunningham, p17t: Shutterstock/Dominionart, p18: Shutterstock/Gorodenkoff, p19: Shutterstock/ Andrea Izzotti, p20: Shutterstock/Everett Collection, p21tl: Shutterstock/Fotokita, p21tr: Shutterstock/DreamArt123, p22: Shutterstock/Zef Art, p23: Shutterstock/Roberto Politi, p24: Shutterstock/Zef Art, p25: Shutterstock/Everett Collection, p26: Shutterstock/ mRGB, p27: Shutterstock/Illustrissima, p28: Shutterstock/Fotokita, p29: Shutterstock/ PhotoFires, p30: Shutterstock/KathySG, p31: Shutterstock/Patsuda Paramee, p33b: Shutterstock/Artem Avetisyan, p33t: Shutterstock/Lario Tus, p35: Shutterstock/S Sokolov, p36: Shutterstock/Patrick Foto, p37: Shutterstock/Christophe Klebert, p38: Shutterstock/Victoria OM, p39: Shutterstock/Everett Collection, p40: Shutterstock/Colin D Young, p41: Shutterstock/CassielMx, p42l: Shutterstock/Fotokitav, p42r: Shutterstock/ Raw Films, p43: Shutterstock/Nadiia Kalameiets, p44: Shutterstock/Danai Khampiranon, p45: Shutterstock/FilipPhotography.

Printed in China

CONTENTS

CHAPTER 1

THINGS THAT GO BUMP IN THE NIGHT

It's the dead of night… A door creaks open, eerily slowly. The air suddenly feels cold, as if all the life and warmth have been sucked out of it. A strange moaning sound echoes through the walls. Something crashes to the floor. Did it fall? Or was it pushed? People who have heard bumps in the night say these are some of the creepy signs that their house is haunted—someone who is no longer alive is visiting them.

Visitors from Another World?

A ghost is the **spirit** of a dead person that some people believe appears to those who are alive. Ghosts are sometimes described as pale, almost transparent, or see-through, versions of their previous, living selves. The locations where these spirits are seen are said to be haunted by their spooky presence. These haunted places can be anything, from woodlands to grand mansions. Ghosts are thought to linger in another form when they come back to visit us. There are many different ideas about why they might do that, but we don't really know if ghosts exist or why they visit living people.

Do you believe in ghosts? There are many stories of mysterious things that go bump in the night…

Do images like this really show a ghostly presence or are they fakes created to trick people?

Fakes and Hoaxes

People have tried to find evidence, or proof, of hauntings through photos, videos, and recordings. Many of these have simply proven there were **logical** explanations for a lot of the events. Sometimes, the evidence discovered has turned out to be a fake or hoax. People might set up a hoax for fun, to get fame, or to make money, for example, by selling tickets to visit their "haunted" home.

Spooky Tales

So, if we don't really have proof that ghosts and haunted places are real, why do so many people believe in them? Maybe it's just that many of us love a good ghost story or a spooky tale, especially on Halloween. Many people around the world truly believe they have seen a ghost or completely believe in the existence of spooks. And there are new sightings of phantoms, or ghosts, every year. Could there be some truth in these terrifying tales?

SET TO SPOOK!

In this book, we are going to explore some of the most mystifying and unsettling reports about ghosts and haunted places. You'll hear about entire armies of ghosts, haunted prisons, and strange spirits. Some of the stories will send shivers down your spine. Some of them will leave you truly spooked!

Ancient Sightings

The idea of ghostly presences and haunted places has troubled people since ancient times. The reason that many ancient peoples had complicated **burial ceremonies** was not just to honor their dead. It was also because they feared the dead would return to haunt them if the bodies weren't buried correctly.

In ancient Egypt, people believed that if the dead were buried incorrectly, they wouldn't pass into the **afterlife**. Instead, the lost souls would wander Earth in misery forever more.

Hungry Ghosts

The earliest stories in ancient China were ghost stories. There are tales of ghosts haunting a house where people once lived, haunting relatives, or even asking strangers for help. Some of these were the ghosts of people who had not been buried by following the proper **rituals**. Some were of people who had suffered a bad or painful death. Hungry ghosts were the spirits of people who were never satisfied with what they had while they were alive, they always wanted more. **Legends** say that if a living person saw a hungry ghost and did not give them food, that person would be cursed.

A lot of movies feature terrifying mummies that have returned from the dead! The ancient Egyptians believed that the dead could come back to terrify them if they were not carefully buried.

A Fishy Fiend

There are stories of a number of different types of ghost, or bhoot, in ancient India. In Bengal, the most haunted places were marshes, ponds, and forests. Mechho bhoots, or fishy ghosts, are male ghosts. They are mainly ghosts of fishermen or others who died by drowning. They are known for their love of fish. They haunt lakes and ponds where they whine, beg, and steal for a piece of fish.

Died in Chains?

There is a famous ghost story from ancient Greece, too. A man named Athenodorus rented a house haunted by a ghost that dragged a heavy chain as it wandered at night. Athenodorus decided to follow the ghost. When he did so, the ghost led him to a place in the courtyard of the house. Then the ghost vanished. Athenodorus ordered the site to be dug up. He discovered the skeleton of a man tied up in chains. After the skeleton was buried the ghost was never seen again.

SPOOKED!

There is a theory that the practice of cremation, or burning a dead body, started because some people thought it was a way of preventing the spirit of a dead person from returning to Earth.

Was Athenodorus really haunted by a strange, chained ghost?

Stories vary throughout Latin America but one constant is that the Weeping Woman always appears to be dressed in a long, white, wet dress.

Mythical Spirits

Around the world, there are still **mythical** ghosts that haunt people's dreams and their waking hours. Tales of these spooky creatures are often told to scare children into staying away from dangerous places, such as lonely woodlands, or to strike fear into people's hearts so that they behave in a certain way. For example, some legends say that those who do not treat their families well will see a mean and dangerous spirit that will teach them a lesson.

The Weeping Woman

In Spanish "la Llorona" means "the Weeping Woman." La Llorona is a famous spirit throughout Latin America that roams rivers and creeks, wailing into the night. The story goes that she is the spirit of a mother who drowned her children and spends forever looking for them. Children are warned not to go out in the dark and wander too close to waterways, for fear that La Llorona might kidnap, or snatch, them and toss them into the river or lake to die in a watery grave.

The Banshee's Cry

According to Irish legend, the Banshee is the spirit of a woman who appears outside a home and screams or wails. The Banshee is said to bring bad news and is often taken to be a sign that someone in a house will soon die. Some believe that she means well and that she simply wants to give family members time to say goodbye to the relative who is about to pass away.

Shape Shifters

According to Scottish legend, a kelpie is a **shape-shifting** spirit that haunts rivers and streams. It sometimes takes the form of a horse that drags children who climb on its back into the river to die. Some kelpies take the shape of a beautiful young woman who tries to lure young men to a watery grave. Other kelpies look like a man with seaweed in his hair or hooves instead of hands, who crushes people in his strong grip.

SPOOKED!

Could some myths and legends have been created to keep people safe, for example, warning children to keep away from rushing rivers at night? Or given how many sightings of these ghosts have been reported, do you think there could be some truth in the tales?

Banshees are famous for their wailing cries.

INVESTIGATING

MYSTERIOUS PHOTOS

Spooky Snaps

The first photographs capturing images of ghosts or spooky spirits were taken not long after cameras and photography were invented. From the 1850s onward, some strange snaps started to appear that seemed to show the ghosts of loved and lost ones standing behind or near their living relatives as they posed for their photographs. It was mysterious...

Ghosts Through a Lens

A US photographer, William Mumler, was one of the first people to capture a ghost in a photograph. In the early 1860s, one of his photos seemed to contain the shadowy outline of his dead cousin. News spread of Mumler's strange ability and soon, people who had lost someone they loved were asking Mumler to take their photographs, too.

In one of Mumler's most famous photographs, the "ghost" of Abraham Lincoln stands behind an image of his wife Mary Todd Lincoln.

A Fluke or a Spook?

Mumler became famous and started to make a lot of money taking photos for families whose relatives had been killed in the Civil War (1861–1865). They all wanted to see their loved ones once again and feel some kind of connection to those they had lost. It was to Mumler's great advantage.

Figures in images can be easily blurred to seem ghostly...

Looking for the Lost

More than 620,000 people died during the Civil War. It is not surprising that some of these grieving relatives looked for connections to their lost loved ones. Soon, people called mediums claimed they could help the living speak with the dead. Photographers like Mumler gave people the chance to see lost sons, husbands, or brothers one last time.

Hounded as a Hoaxer

Eventually, some people became concerned that Mumler was a fake who was cruelly charging grieving people for his images. Then the circus showman P.T. Barnum accused Mumler of breaking into people's houses to steal photos of their dead relatives in order to make his spirit photographs. Mumler was put on trial for fraud and Barnum spoke against him.

Exposed as a Fake

During his trial, other photographers described different ways Mumler could have made it look like his photos captured spirits. They even showed the court a hoax photograph to prove how easy it was to make a spirit image. The photo showed Barnum with the "ghost" of Abraham Lincoln. Despite the allegations, the case was dismissed because of a lack of evidence, but Mumler's career was over.

CHAPTER 2

BACK FROM THE DEAD

Some ghosts are said to be of people who return from the dead after being unfairly executed, or put to death, or cruelly murdered. Perhaps these ghosts cannot rest until those who put them to death have been punished? Even if this isn't the case, the stories of their deaths and murders still make for grim and spine-tingling reading!

Terror in the Tower

The Tower of London, in the United Kingdom (UK), has been the place of gruesome **executions** in history. The most famous was of Anne Boleyn, who became King Henry VIII's second wife in 1533. Anne gave birth to a daughter but Henry was angry that she had failed to give him the son and **heir** he wanted. So, in 1536, he accused Anne of cheating on him and imprisoned her in the Tower of London. Anne was **beheaded** in the grounds of the Tower.

Tales of Horror

There have been many sightings of Anne Boleyn's ghost haunting the Tower of London. In 1864, a soldier on patrol said he questioned a strange figure in white who refused to answer him. He plunged his **bayonet** into the figure but to his horror, the weapon went straight through the ghostly woman!

The man who beheaded Anne Boleyn struck off her head with a single swing of his sharpened sword. Sometimes, Anne's ghost is said to be headless too.

SPOOKED!

There are regular reports of people seeing and hearing the ghost of the fifth wife of Henry VIII, Catherine Howard, in Hampton Court Palace. There are other eerie events too. In 1999, during two separate tours in one day, two female visitors fainted in an area known as the Haunted Gallery.

When darkness falls over Hampton Court Palace, it's not hard to imagine that you might see someone or something lurking in the spooky shadows.

Catherine the Screaming Queen

Henry VIII was more than 30 years older than Catherine Howard when she became his fifth wife. At some point, Catherine fell in love with another man. When Henry found out, Catherine was arrested and sent to Hampton Court Palace to await her trial. When she was first arrested, Catherine broke free of her guards. She ran down the corridor, screaming for mercy from the king. She didn't make it to the chapel where Henry was praying because the guards caught up with her. She was sent to the Tower of London to await her dreadful **fate**.

The Haunted Gallery

The terrified girl was only a teenager when she was beheaded at the Tower of London in 1542. Today, Catherine's ghost is said to torment people in the Haunted Gallery. They say her ghost runs along the corridor, wailing and asking Henry for forgiveness, desperate to avoid the horrible death that was to come.

A World of Witches

During the **Middle Ages**, some people were accused of being witches. It was said that they worked with the devil and had dangerous magical powers. It took only two people who disliked you, owed you money, or had another problem with you to accuse you of being a witch, and you could be put on trial. One test to figure out if someone was a witch involved lowering a woman into a pond. If she floated, she was a witch and should be executed. If she drowned, she wasn't a witch —but was dead anyway. People float in water, so most of those tested as witches were found guilty and put to death.

Unable to Rest?

In June, 1749, even a **nun** was beheaded. Maria Renata Singer was beheaded near the Marienberg **fortress** above the beautiful city of Würzburg, Germany, and her body burned. Nuns at her **convent** had been getting sick and some feared that they were being possessed, or taken over by the devil. Someone accused Maria of witchcraft, so she was executed. To this day, her angry ghost is said to roam the halls of the fortress and her old convent.

During the Middle Ages, many people believed that groups of witches met to perform witchcraft and flew on broomsticks!

SPOOKED!

Are the places where people were tormented and murdered as witches haunted, or do people think that they see spirits there because of the horrible stories associated with these places?

A witch's bridle was a cruel and horrible device used to torture women accused of witchcraft. It stopped them from speaking and caused great pain.

The Torture of Bald Agnes

Agnes Sampson was a midwife—a nurse who helps women give birth. She was also a natural healer, or someone who uses plants to help people feel better. She lived in Scotland, UK, in the late sixteenth century. Agnes was so good at her job that, unfortunately, some people thought she must have **supernatural** powers. At the time, Scotland was a very superstitious place, and Agnes was soon accused of working for the devil. When she refused to admit to being a witch, Agnes was taken to a dungeon. Her hair was shaved off, she was fixed against a wall by a painful contraption known as a witch's bridle, and partly strangled.

Tormented to This Day

Agnes finally gave in and she "confessed." She was taken from her cell, tied to a pole, and slowly burned until she was dead. The ghost of Agnes Sampson is now said to roam the halls of the Palace of Holyroodhouse in Edinburgh, beaten, bloodied, and bald. Sometimes, she is seen floating in mid-air toward people with outstretched arms.

INVESTIGATING

SPOOKY SALEM

Spooky Salem Witch Trials

In January 1692, several young girls became sick in Salem Village, Massachusetts, and no one knew why. People were scared and started to panic when there were suggestions that the sickness had been caused by witchcraft. Church ministers encouraged followers to find the people in their midst who were responsible for the evil. The result was the Salem Witch Trials, the most famous witch trials in US history.

The Devil's Magic

In 1692, life in Massachusetts was ruled by religion. It was against the law not to go to church. **Puritans** believed that the devil was real and that he used witches to do his evil work. They believed that witches who worshiped the devil could cause bad weather, ruin harvests, harm children, turn into animals, and fly in the air. They called witchcraft the devil's magic.

Wrongful Accusations

Life in Massachusetts in the seventeenth century was strict and harsh. People lived in fear of starvation and of dying in battles with their Native American neighbors and rival French settlers. They wanted someone to blame for their problems. Whether out of real fear or out of meanness and **resentment** toward neighbors they disliked, the Salem villagers accused more than 200 people of practicing witchcraft.

The Salem Witch Trials were very dramatic, with scenes of fainting and outbursts from the gathered crowds. John Hathorne was a judge at the Trials. He was said to be determined to convict people of witchcraft. He refused to even consider that the accused could truly be innocent.

Some people think that the ghosts of witches said to haunt Old Burying Point Cemetery in Salem, came back from the dead to torment their killer: Judge Hathorne.

Terrible Trials

The trials were a cruel sham. Imagine being accused of something you did not do. If you said you were innocent, you would most likely be found guilty and executed anyway. If you gave a confession and said you were guilty and apologized, you may have been set free. Most of the accused people chose to confess, but a total of 19 people: 14 women, 5 men, and even 2 dogs were put to death.

Haunted by Horror

Some say that this horrible history still haunts the town of Salem. There are reports of the ghosts of victims wandering through the local cemetery. People have heard spirit voices crying out, and seen strange lights. Visitors report feeling sudden drops in temperature as they walk through the cemetery grounds.

CHAPTER 3

ARMIES OF THE DEAD

Terrible or sudden deaths are often believed to cause ghosts, and few deaths are more **traumatic** than those on the battlefield. The devastation caused when soldiers die in bloody battles and kill enemies in brutal encounters is so awful that it leaves an unforgettable mark on our world.

The Ghost March

In the Middle Ages, there was more than one story of troops of spirits traveling without rest. One of these armies in torment was witnessed by a priest named Walchelin in 1091. As Walchelin walked home one night in Normandy, France, he heard what he thought must be an army approaching, so he hid behind a tree. He watched as thousands of people passed by, including a large group of knights. Walchelin recognized some of the people, including his own brother. He realized this was the legendary army of the dead. The story says that the army was made up of people who had done bad things when they were alive. They were being punished by having to continue a never-ending march.

Battles of the Middle Ages were gruesome. Could the sites at which they took place be haunted because of the trauma that happened there?

SPOOKED!

When large numbers of people die in one battle or on one battlefield, people often say that they can still hear the eerie screams, cannons firing, the thunder of hooves, and battle cries in those areas for centuries afterward.

This painting of the Battle of Little Bighorn was made by a Cheyenne Native American. It shows the terrible fighting that took place. Perhaps it is no surprise that Little Bighorn is said to be haunted after such violence took place there.

A Fight to the Death

The Battle of Little Bighorn is a legendary battle fought between the US Army and a group of Native American tribes in 1876. The battle was fought near the banks of the Little Bighorn River in Montana. It is also known as Custer's Last Stand because, rather than retreat, or leave, General Custer and his men stood their ground. They eventually lost and all were killed. Today, the site is said to be filled with screaming and groans. According to many visitors and local people, the warriors who died there are restless.

Other-Worldly Warriors

Visitors to the cemetery and battlefields there claim to have heard and seen the ghosts of US Army soldiers and Native American warriors fighting. They say they hear the soft murmuring of eerie voices and the battle cries of Indian warriors charging on horseback. People who walk through the cemetery that contains graves of many of the fallen soldiers, speak of cold spots that seem to spring up from nowhere. There have been reports of people seeing soldiers and warriors fighting to the death.

A Watery Grave

The story of the USS *Arizona* ship will send shivers down your spine before there is even a mention of ghosts... On December 7, 1941, the ship was at the naval base at Pearl Harbor, Hawaii, when Japanese forces attacked. After the ship was bombed, weapons and fuel on board caught fire and created a massive explosion. As the ship sank beneath the water, it was struck by more bombs. More than 1,170 crewmen died. Because of the fire and the twisted metal of the ruined ship, it was impossible to bring back the bodies of the dead crewmen. Instead, they were left on board.

A Haunted Tomb

The wreckage of the USS *Arizona* became a **mass tomb** and underwater graveyard. A large concrete **memorial** was built over the remains of the sunken battleship and its dead. After such a terrible loss of life, it's maybe no surprise to learn that the surrounding area is said to be haunted. There have been reports of strange events, sounds, and presences. People hear footsteps and voices, see household objects moved by ghosts, and shadows creeping along walls and ceilings. Visitors often report feeling a sense of panic and seeing a strange mist floating up and down.

Along with other US Navy ships, the USS *Arizona* was devastated during the attack on Pearl Harbor.

The USS *Hornet* is considered to be the most haunted ship in the US Navy.

The Old Gray Ghost

The USS *Hornet* is nicknamed the Old Gray Ghost. This could be because it was the latest in a long line of US Navy ships named Hornet, and so carried the spirits of all the men who served aboard other Hornet boats in the past. This historic aircraft carrier was built in the 1940s. It fought major battles in the Pacific during World War II (1939–1945), and served during the Korean War (1950–1953) and the Vietnam War (1955–1975). Today, USS *Hornet*, is a museum, but it is also known for being a center of some very scary supernatural activity.

The Spookiest Ship

One of the spookiest places in the USS *Hornet* is an old hospital below deck, where many suffered and died. All sorts of spooky happenings occur there. There are reports of unexplainable shadowy figures and footsteps. Light switches turn on, locker doors open, and objects move by themselves. The sound of an old music box suddenly fills the empty corridors.

SPOOKED!

Volunteers who work in the USS *Hornet* museum in Alameda, California, often demonstrate to visitors how flashlights will spookily turn on and off by themselves when left alone. Some volunteers claim ghosts will "talk" with them by turning on a flashlight to answer yes to questions they ask!

The Horrors of War

In Northern Ireland, there is a building called Craigavon House. During World War I (1914–1918), Craigavon House was turned into a hospital for severely injured soldiers who arrived home in large numbers. It specialized in caring for servicemen who were also shell-shocked. This is a mental and emotional health problem caused by the horror of war. Today, it is called Post Traumatic Stress Disorder, or PTSD. The soldiers at Craigavon House were encouraged to relax in the leafy grounds and work in the garden. Later, the house became a home and place to recover for men who had fought in World War I and II.

A Haunted Hospital

The men who stayed at the house suffered unspeakable trauma. Today, the ghosts of soldiers who died in the house after suffering life-threatening injuries on the battlefield are said to haunt Craigavon House. People have heard loud moans or even faint whispers that seem to come from one of the mirrors hanging on the walls. Others have heard the sound of a woman's heels moving along the top corridor and the smell of lavender. Perhaps this is the ghost of the nurse who ran the hospital, still watching over her patients?

Do the ghosts of traumatized soldiers live out their horrors on the battlefield at Craigavon House?

Secrets in the Rock

Deep within the massive cliff known as the Rock of Gibraltar off the coast of Spain, there is a maze of deep tunnels and chambers. The British Army dug many of these spaces during World War II in which to safely store food, weapons, and equipment. There were sleeping barracks and a hospital too. Hidden deep in the rock, soldiers and supplies would be safe from attacks by German planes and ships.

Tormented Tunnels

Some men died digging the tunnels within the Rock of Gibraltar during World War II. Their ghosts refuse to be forgotten. Visitors to the site have heard whistling, digging, and the sound of men singing as they work. One visitor felt someone tugging at his shirt and an invisible force jerking him backward.

SPOOKED!

The Stay Behind Cave was a top-secret chamber. If the Nazis captured Gibraltar, six British volunteers would be sealed inside this cave with enough supplies for a year. They would spy on the enemy from two small holes and radio regular reports to London. If one of the men died, the others were to cement his body in a wall or under the floor. Gibraltar never fell to the Germans.

INVESTIGATING

THE BATTLEFIELD

Ghostly Soldiers

Gettysburg, Pennsylvania is considered to be one of the most haunted places in the United States, if not the world. It is the location of one of the biggest and deadliest battles of the Civil War. Some people believe the nightmare of that battle never ended for some of the soldiers who were killed there. Across the old battlefields and even in the town, it is said that ghosts of the fallen still roam.

A Bloody and Brutal Battle

The battle was terrible and long-lasting. Fighting raged back and forth and by the end of the three terrible days, the battlefields were littered with bodies. In the brutal battle of Gettysburg, more than 7,000 men were killed and 46,000 were injured or missing. It is known as the turning point of the Civil War.

Local Legends

Many modern-day residents of Gettysburg say that they can still feel the presence of those who lost their lives during that battle. Some say that around the town they have heard footsteps, felt cold spots, and seen shadows they can't explain. There are some places they simply won't go.

Strange Sights and Sounds

Visitors to the battlefields and those who work there report seeing shadows in the corner of an eye and feeling chills down the spine. There are tales of ghostly soldiers, phantom horsemen, faces, and figures mysteriously appearing in photographs that tourists take. Sometimes, the sounds of mysterious footsteps, the groaning of wounded soldiers, or the shouts of orders issued in the midst of battle are heard. People even say they smell tobacco smoke—when no one is smoking...

Do ghosts of the fallen still haunt the Gettysburg battlefield?

The Battle of Gettysburg took place from July 1 to 3 in 1863. Today, it is often reenacted.

Devil's Den

Devil's Den is a ridge covered with boulders that became the site of a particularly high number of casualties on the second day of the Battle of Gettysburg. More than 1,800 men were killed, wounded, captured, or went missing there. As well as strange sightings, people also say that camera equipment and other electronic gadgets sometimes stop working near this sad and spooky location.

Ghost Filming

In 2020, a tourist said he captured video footage of ghosts during a late-night tour of the battle site in Gettysburg. As he drove along, he started hearing noises and saw a strange fog. He said he filmed shapes "the size of humans" moving in the darkness. Were these figures simply reflections made as his car headlights shone on nearby cannons at the site, or were they something far more spooky?

CHAPTER 4

HAUNTED HOUSES

One of the most common features of many spooky movies is the creepy haunted house. Such horrible homes often stand alone or at the end of a street, looking neglected, or uncared for, and rundown, but also strangely forbidding. What is it about old houses that sends shivers down our spines and makes us think ghosts hang around to haunt them?

Secrets Within Their Walls

Most haunted houses are linked to some type of legend. It usually involves a story about a gruesome accident or death, or a history of **suicide** and murder. One of the common signs of a haunted house is a strange smell that people cannot explain. Another is a sudden change in temperature when there are no drafts, or a weird sensation running down the back of your neck...

The Most Haunted House in England?

One of the most haunted houses in England, UK, was mysteriously burned by a fire in 1939. As the fire blazed behind the windows of Borley Rectory in Essex, witnesses said they saw the shadows of mysterious ghostly figures in the background.

Maybe you do not believe in haunted houses, but would you like to spend the night alone in a creepy old building like this one?

SPOOKED!

Are large, drafty old houses more likely to be haunted than other places? Are the rattling, creaking sounds in upstairs rooms, the sighing and moaning of wind passing through cracks, curtains waving in a breeze, echoes, and cold spots just features of an old building, or are they signs of something spookily supernatural?

Murdered for Love?

Borley Rectory was built as a home for pastors, or church ministers, in the middle of the nineteenth century on the site of an old **abbey**. Soon after the abbey had been built, there was talk of people seeing the ghost of a nun and other spooky events. Then, bells began to ring and objects were thrown around. According to local legend, a **monk** and nun had run away together in the thirteenth century. After they were caught, the monk was hanged and the poor distraught nun was left to die in the convent.

Frightened and Fearful

Pastors who came to live in the Rectory were often scared away. One claimed to see a headless man in the garden. Another saw strange writing scrawled on the walls. The house would suddenly fill with strange smells, objects vanished and reappeared, bells rang, and peculiar voices were heard. Only after the house was demolished, did the strange events finally come to an end.

The Brown Lady of Raynham Hall

The Brown Lady of Raynham Hall is a ghost that is said to haunt Raynham Hall in Norfolk, England. The ghost got her name from the brown dress it is claimed she wears. The Brown Lady made Raynham Hall one of the most famous haunted houses in the UK.

Locked Up Until the End of Her Days

Raynham Hall is a grand, old English country home. The Brown Lady of Raynham Hall is believed to be the ghost of Lady Dorothy Walpole. She was the second wife of Charles Townshend, who was known to have a terrible temper. The story goes that Dorothy fell in love with another man and when Townshend found out, he locked her up in rooms in Raynham Hall. He never allowed her to leave, even to see her beloved children. Dorothy stayed there until she died from a disease called smallpox in 1726.

The Green Lady of Brissac

The Château de Brissac is a huge castle in France's Loire Valley. Its charming appearance hides a terrible truth. The Château is supposedly haunted by the tragic figure of the Green Lady, who wears the same green dress she had on the night she was murdered.

If ghosts like the Brown Lady of Raynham Hall exist, they must be terrifying to encounter.

A Double Murder

The Green Lady is the ghost of Charlotte, the daughter of King Charles VII. She married the owner of the castle, Jacques de Brézé, but was unhappy there. She was used to busy palace life and she disliked the drafty country castle and her husband, who spent most of his time hunting. Charlotte fell in love with another man. When her husband found out, he killed them both in a terrible fit of rage.

A Scary Sight

The Green Lady is often seen in the tower room of the castle's chapel in her green dress. The sound of her wailing is heard throughout the castle in the early hours of the morning. She roams the rooms, scaring many guests. However, the most alarming thing about the Green Lady is her face. Those who claim to have seen her say that there are gaping holes where her eyes and nose should be.

Beautiful though the Château is, its terrifying story shrouds the building in horror.

SPOOKED!

Many people claim to have seen the ghost of the Brown Lady walking the halls of the house, never to escape. One report claimed the phantom even had dark and empty eye sockets in her eerily glowing face.

The Crawleys of Monte Cristo

Christopher William Crawley was a rich farmer and landowner who built the Monte Cristo Homestead in Australia in 1885. He lived in this grand house with his wife, their seven children, and many servants. The family entertained the wealthiest people in their town. Behind the glamor, however, lay devastation and dark secrets.

Death at the Homestead

Death seemed to hover over the house. A young maid is said to have fallen to her death from the second-story balcony. Some people see the outline of a female figure on the balcony and hear her footsteps walking up and down in the dark depths of the night. The Crawley's youngest daughter, a 10-month-old baby, died when her nanny dropped her down the stairs. Some believe this was on purpose, while others say it was an accident.

The Monte Cristo Homestead is said to be the most haunted house in Australia. Even if you don't believe in ghosts, it is a spooky reminder of the place's grisly past and the sad end that came to some of the people who lived there.

The Haunting of the Homestead

After the last members of the Crawley family left in 1948, the Monte Cristo Homestead remained empty and became run down. In 1963, the Ryan family moved in. They said that they soon had many spine-tingling experiences. They saw figures in old-fashioned clothes and felt cold hands on their shoulders. Their names were called out when no one was there. They heard strange voices in the distance, and footsteps in the hallways.

The House of Horror

A house in Amityville, New York, looked every inch the Lutz family's dream house when they bought it in 1975. So why, after just 28 days, did they flee from it and never look back? The horrible truth was that the year before they moved in, a young man shot six members of his family there.

A Family in Fear

The Lutz family claimed the house was haunted. They said swarms of flies suddenly appeared in winter. They said cabinets mysteriously slammed shut, slime oozed from ceilings, and beds lifted into the air. The front door would open and shut in the middle of the night and the house felt cold for days on end. George Lutz woke up at 3:15 a.m. nearly every day—the same time that the murders happened...

Did ghostly figures really haunt the house in Amityville? Some people believe that the terrifying stories are true.

SPOOKED!

Was the story of Amityville a horror or a hoax? The Lutz's attorney said he helped the couple come up with the lies, but for his entire life, George Lutz said it was all true. A team of **paranormal** investigators said they felt an evil force in the house and even took a photo of a ghostly boy peering out from a bedroom.

INVESTIGATING

THE WHITE HOUSE

Feet-Nibbling Pets

In 2009, Michelle Obama told school children visiting the White House that she and her husband President Barack Obama sometimes heard strange sounds in the corridors at night. Other members of the Obama family have said they sometimes sensed something invisible nibbling at their feet. Ghosts of long-dead White House pets are just some of many spooks that are said to lurk in the White House, the most famous home in the United States.

The Ghost of Abraham Lincoln

The most well-known ghost to haunt the White House is that of President Abraham Lincoln. A whole host of famous people have claimed to have seen Lincoln in the White House or experienced spooky sensations in his rooms. British Prime Minister Winston Churchill said he saw Lincoln's ghost when he stayed in the Lincoln Bedroom. Lincoln was assassinated, or killed, in 1865. He never slept in that bedroom but he did use it as an office. Ronald Reagan, president of the United States from 1981 until 1989, said his dog barked uncontrollably whenever he was outside the Lincoln Bedroom, and the dog would never enter it.

Lincoln's Son

If any US president were to haunt the White House, people say Lincoln would be the most likely. He himself believed in ghosts and took part in two rituals with his wife, held at the White House, to try to contact their dead son. Lincoln was brutally assassinated—he was shot in the head while watching a play. Like many ghosts, Lincoln had unfinished business, and died before his time.

A Gathering of Ghosts

But, it's not just Lincoln's ghost that wanders the White House. Ghosts of many other people are said to have appeared there on different occasions. Abigail Adams, wife of John Adams, president from 1797 to 1801, is still reported to hang out the laundry in the East Room. Thomas Jefferson, president from 1801 to 1809, is heard playing his violin in the Yellow Oval Room. The ghost of Dolley Madison, the wife of James Madison, president from 1809 to 1817, is said to wander around the Rose Garden, checking on the bushes she originally planted there.

Could the White House and other old houses that are steeped in history be haunted by the people who once lived there?

CHAPTER 5

HALLS OF HORRORS

Large abandoned buildings that once held a lot of people, but are now empty, are some of the places that claim to be most haunted. This is especially true of places such as prisons and hospitals, which once housed troubled people. Or perhaps the fact that many people lived in or visited these halls of horror simply increases the chances that something tragic happened in them?

Buildings That Remember?

Some people believe that when extreme pain and suffering happen in a place, they affect the mood of the building. Those who caused some sort of disturbance or impression remain there. The hauntings that take place in many of these locations are like reruns of the tragic event or series of events that happened there in the past. These locations store up imprints of sights and sounds from the past and replay them later.

A Prison with a Past

In the nineteenth century, prisoners in the Eastern State Penitentiary in Philadelphia, Pennsylvania, lived alone for 23 hours a day in a private cell. Guards passed meals through a small hole, and prisoners were allowed to exercise in a yard for an hour a day. They weren't allowed to speak and wore black hoods outside their cells to ensure they could not see other inmates. This total **isolation** was meant to give dangerous criminals the chance to think about the terrible things they had done.

Tales of Torture

If prisoners tried to talk to each other, punishments were tough. A prisoner's hands were chained behind his back and an iron **gag** fitted over his tongue. The gag was attached to the chains on his wrists. Prisoners were starved or dunked in ice-cold baths. They were bound so tightly in the so-called Mad Chair, it cut off their circulation.

Spooks in the Cells

Many prisoners took their own lives and others were driven crazy by the place. No wonder visitors today report feeling a negative, horrible energy in the cells. Visitors to the prison say they see shadowy figures and ghostly faces and hear mysterious weeping, whispering, and cackling sounds echo through the creepy corridors.

SPOOKED!

Some people say that ghosts seem to appear after the start of repairs or renovations in an old building. They think that knocking down walls releases that energy or those spirits in a haunted place.

Many people travel to haunted places hoping to capture evidence or see spirits.

Welcome to the Haunted Hotel

Sometimes, the places that should be most welcoming are quite the opposite… The Banff Springs hotel in Alberta looks quaint and cozy, but don't let that fool you. Rumor has it that this is one of the most haunted buildings in Canada. When guests arrive, some say they are shown to their room by a **bellhop** named Sam McCauley. Sam worked at the hotel 50 years ago but his ghost still likes to help, often turning on lights and opening locked doors.

Terrifying Tales

There are other terrifying reports connected to this hotel. Some people say they have spotted a strange woman on the stairs or dancing in the ballroom. The unusual thing is that flames flare from the back of her dress. Could this be the ghost of a bride who broke her neck when she tumbled down the staircase in a panic after her dress caught fire?

Shut and Sealed

Another Banff legend is of a family that was murdered in Room 873. The door to this room has since been sealed but some guests say they have seen the souls who lost their lives there in the hallway.

At The Stanley Hotel (see opposite), guests report hearing children's laughter and the children running down the halls. They even feel someone playing with their hair.

Staff reassure guests that The Stanley Hotel ghosts are friendly, or maybe they don't exist at all, but would you risk staying here?

Unwanted Guests?

There are creepy stories of people hearing strange voices, being touched by someone they cannot see, and many other very spooky happenings at the The Stanley Hotel in Colorado. This grand 142-room hotel in the Rocky Mountains was opened by Freelan Oscar Stanley in 1909, after he had stayed in the area to recover from a serious illness.

Spooky Sensations

After Freelan and his wife died, there were reports that they never left. His ghost reportedly hovers behind staff at reception, as if checking up on them. His wife's ghost can still be heard tinkling on the piano in the hotel's music room. There are other strange reports of clothes being mysteriously unpacked, lights going on and off, and objects moving on their own.

SPOOKED!

When a maid named Elizabeth Wilson took a lit candle into Room 217 in 1911, where there was a gas leak, the place exploded. The maid was thrown down an entire story and was lucky to survive. She died in the 1950s and her ghost is said to haunt Room 217, which she sometimes tidies overnight while guests are sleeping!

INVESTIGATING

THE HOSPITAL

Spooky Sanatorium

During the 1800s and early 1900s, entire families and, sometimes, whole towns in the United States were wiped out by tuberculosis, or TB, a deadly disease of the lungs. Many called it the "white death." In 1926, a massive five-story TB hospital called the Waverly Hills Sanatorium opened on a windswept hill in Louisville, Kentucky. Tragically, most of the thousands of patients went to the hospital to be treated never left it.

Do the ghosts of people who died in the sanatorium haunt it to this day?

Terrible Treatments

To stop the spread of TB, patients who came to the hospital could not see their families or loved ones. Even the children who were forced to stay there rarely saw their parents. Some of the treatments given there were appalling. Patients were forced to sit for long spells in the fresh air, even in heavy snow or howling gales. Some people were operated on. Balloons were fitted in some patient's lungs and then filled with air to expand them. Muscles and ribs were removed from patients' chests to allow their lungs to let in more air. These surgeries were often a last resort and unsurprisingly, caused many painful deaths.

The Body Chute

Estimates of the number of patients who died in the hospital range from 6,000 to 50,000. To avoid upsetting other patients, doctors got rid of the bodies down a body chute. This was an enclosed tunnel that used a cable system to lower bodies from the hospital to waiting trains on railroad tracks at the bottom of the hill.

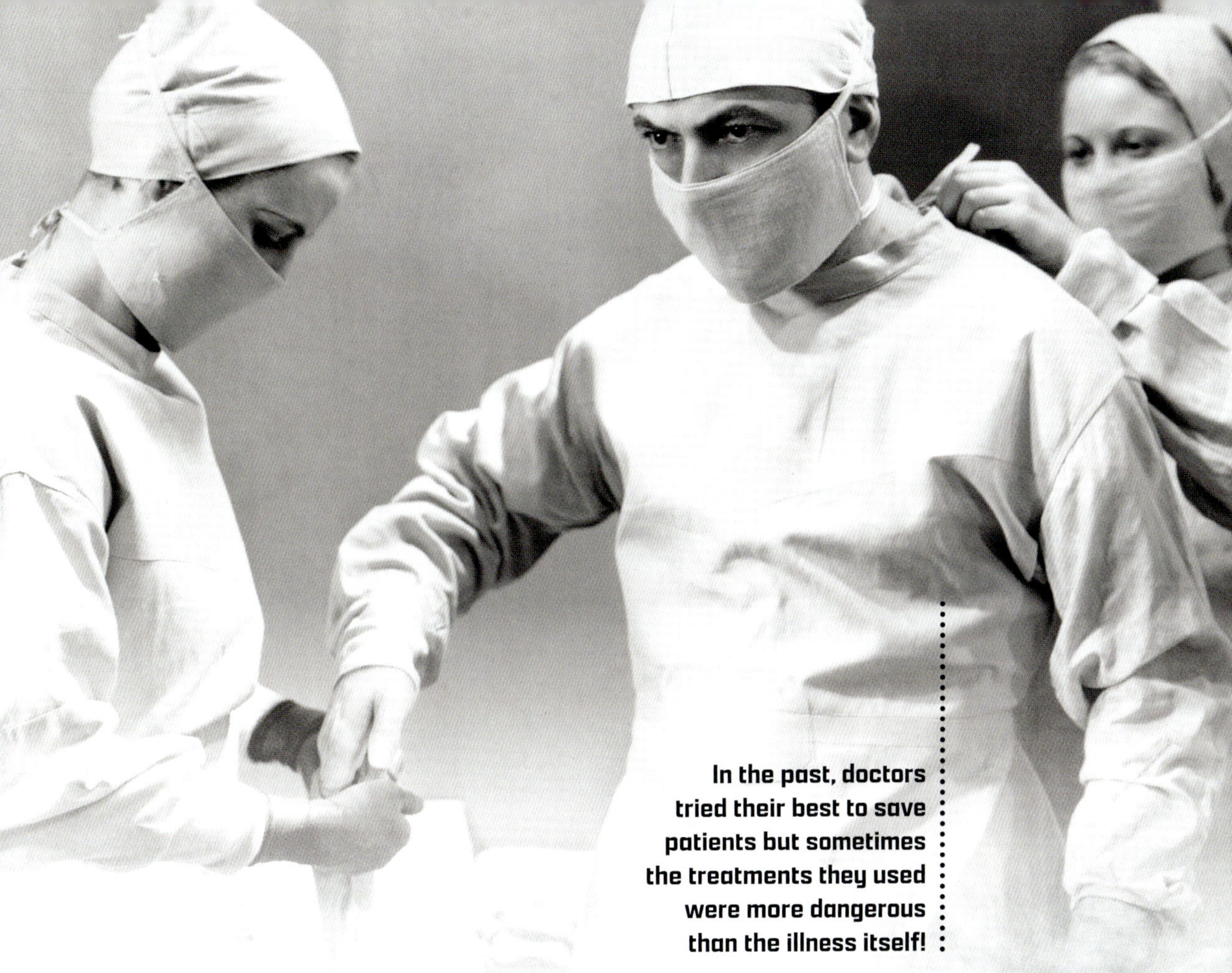

In the past, doctors tried their best to save patients but sometimes the treatments they used were more dangerous than the illness itself!

Spooks of the Sanatorium

Waverly Hills was closed in 1961, but many visitors say they see spooks from the sanatorium. There have been sightings of a little girl running up and down the third floor, and a little boy rolling a ball at visitors and waiting for them to roll it back. A mysterious man in a white doctor's coat patrols the corridors at night. People say they have heard slamming doors and eerie footsteps. They have seen lights in rooms when there should have been none, and some even claim that they have been slapped by invisible hands!

Room 502

Many stories of the strange and spooky happenings in the sanatorium feature the hospital's Room 502. Two nurses died there in strange circumstances. One is believed to have hanged herself. The other either threw herself from a window or was pushed out of it, and fell to her death. Visitors have seen shapes moving in the windows of Room 502 and ghosts of these tragic nurses are believed to roam the hallways.

CHAPTER 6

ISLANDS OF SPIRITS AND SHADOWS

There are many islands around the world that are tropical paradises and have everything tourists need for a great vacation. Some islands are far from where people live but beautiful homes for wildlife. And then there are the other islands, the islands of spirits and shadows. These are islands that have strange pasts and dark secrets. Islands that fill visitors with a sense of terror.

Smoke and Spooks

Crater Lake in Oregon is the clearest and deepest lake in the United States. The area around it has long been home to Native American Klamath tribes. Tribal legends say that there are fearful beings hiding in the water and that Crater Lake was a doorway into the Below-World, or Hell. At night, there are often sightings of eerie smoke billowing up from an island on the lake called Wizard Island. Some people say the sightings are the spirits of the island. They have even reported seeing dragonlike monsters lurking beneath the lake around Wizard Island.

When rangers check on the mysterious campfires spotted on Wizard Island, there is no one there and no scorch marks on the ground.

SPOOKED!

People have also reported seeing strange objects that they describe as **UFOs** flitting in and out of the Crater Lake. Could these be the spirits of Wizard Island?

The Island of the Dolls

An island of dolls sounds fun, but this strange place is anything but fun. The dolls and parts of dolls that dangle from the trees on this small island in Xochimilco, south of Mexico City, are a little creepy in the daytime. But, when darkness falls, the sight of them in the moonlight is pretty scary!

Island Spirits?

In the 1950s, the caretaker of the small island discovered the body of a young girl who had drowned in a nearby canal in strange circumstances. He also found a doll. He hung the doll from a tree in memory of the girl. Soon after this, he said he started to sense spirits following him. So, he attached more and more dolls to the trees as gifts to the spirits that he sensed.

Strange Sightings

Visitors to the island have reported seeing the heads of the dolls turn to follow them. Some legends say the dolls' eyes open sometimes. Other visitors claim to have heard whispers, footsteps, and even wails of spirits echo around the island.

Some people think that the island's caretaker made up the story about the girl because he was lonely. Others say he collected the dolls to protect himself from the spirits he believed lived on the island.

The Plague Island

In the fourteenth century, a terrible disease known as the bubonic plague swept across Europe, killing millions. The isolated island of Poveglia off Italy was chosen as a place to send victims of this cruel disease to die. People were brought there kicking and screaming, because they knew it was a death sentence. It is estimated that up to 160,000 people died on the island and were buried in huge holes that became known as plague pits.

An Island of Ghosts?

Later, in 1922, a hospital was opened on Poveglia. Patients who were suffering mental breakdowns were brought there. When they reported seeing the ghosts of plague victims and said they were kept awake at night by the sound of screaming, they were ignored. The patients also suffered brutal experiments by doctors who were trying to cure them of their insanity. Hand drills have been found in the ruins of the hospital. These made holes in patients' heads, supposedly to let out the madness.

Today, Poveglia Island is deserted. Many people say its only inhabitants are ghosts.

SPOOKED!

The hospital was closed and Poveglia Island abandoned in 1968 when a doctor fell from the highest tower and died. Some say he was driven mad by his patients. Others think he was pushed from the tower.

Island of the Dead

Hart Island, which is located at the western end of Long Island Sound, is known as the Island of the Dead. It certainly has been a place of much misery. During the Civil War there was a prison camp there, where more than 200 prisoners died and were buried. New York City bought the island in 1868, and in 1870, victims of **yellow fever** were sent there to die. After that, there was a women's insane asylum, a TB hospital, a **missile** base, and another prison. Since 1869, more than 1 million people have been buried in unmarked graves on Hart Island. Some were victims of past **epidemics** and there are even victims of Covid-19 there too. Perhaps it is no wonder that many people believe this island is haunted.

Imagination or Infestation?

After reading this book, do you think ghosts and haunted houses are real? Are there really buildings and islands infested with supernatural beings? Or are these sightings and experiences tricks of the light or products of an overactive imagination? Perhaps the histories of these unhappy places make people imagine the spooks and strange events they see there. Could it perhaps be that some people want to see supernatural beings so badly they imagine them?

Will we really find ghosts and haunted places if we go looking for them, or will we simply imagine them?

INVESTIGATING

ALCATRAZ

Tribal Prison

Alcatraz Island is a small island off the coast of San Francisco, California. It is often known as The Rock. Grisly tales and legends of the island have been told for centuries. Long ago, Native Americans of the Ohlone tribe lived on the **mainland** nearby. They believed the island was cursed and evil spirits lived there. They used it as a place to send tribal members who broke laws and deserved the worst punishment. Some were banished for life to die there among the evil spirits.

The Rock

In 1933, an old military prison on the isolated island was turned into a maximum security jail for the very worst criminals. This prison was designed to break the spirits of even the most difficult and hardened criminals that ended up there. **Inmates** who broke the prison's many rules faced harsh punishments. Some were sent to cell 14D, known as "The Hole." This was a cell with a steel door where prisoners could be left for many days, alone and in darkness. The dark room removed what was left of their hope, and many took their own lives there.

Prisoners left alone in cell 14D were tormented by the isolation and darkness.

It is said that the empty cells inside the walls of Alcatraz are still home to the restless ghosts that remain there.

Lurking in the Shadows

Today, the prison is a museum. While the island was still a prison, several guards reported spooky experiences, such as hearing the sounds of sobbing and moaning and sensing terrible smells. Some reported seeing a strange creature with glowing eyes or phantom prisoners and soldiers. Visitors and staff in the museum today say that they have heard, seen, or felt strange spirits lurking in the shadows of the often fog-cloaked island. They say they hear the sounds of men's voices, screams, whistles, and the clanging of metal doors within the walls.

Found Dead

In the 1940s, guards found a prisoner dead on the floor of cell 14D. Legend has it that the night he died, he had been shouting that a creature with glowing eyes was trying to kill him. The guards who found him the following morning, said his dead face looked terrified and that there were hand-prints around his throat. A doctor declared that the prisoner had not strangled himself. Some people believe that the man was killed by the ghost of an evil prisoner who was often seen wandering the corridors. Or was he the victim of one of the ancient evil spirits in the Ohlone tribe legends?

GLOSSARY

abbey a building where monks or nuns live or used to live

afterlife life after death. Some people believe that after we die we go to live in another world

bayonet a long, sharp blade that can be fixed to the end of a rifle

beheaded cut off someone's head, especially as a punishment

bellhop a person paid to carry bags and open doors in a hotel

burial ceremonies formal public funeral events with special traditions

convent a building in which nuns live

epidemics the large-scale spreading of diseases in a relatively short period of time

executions putting criminals to death

fate a mysterious power that some people believe controls what happens in the future

fortress a large, strong building that can be defended from attack

gag a cloth tied over a person's mouth to stop them speaking

heir a person who receives the property or title of someone who dies

inhabitants people who live in a place

isolation being completely alone

legends traditional stories

logical reasonable and sensible

mainland the main part of a country or continent

mass tomb a place where many people are buried together

memorial something created to honor a dead person

Middle Ages the period between CE 476 and about CE 1500

missile a weapon that is sent through the air

monk a man who dedicates his life to his religion

mummies dead bodies that have been preserved

mythical describes a traditional story that explains a natural event

nun a woman who dedicates her life to her religion

paranormal impossible to explain by known natural forces or by science

Puritans a religious group of people who wanted to simplify the Church of England (COE)

resentment a feeling of anger you get if you have to accept something you do not like

rituals actions performed in a certain way, especially as part of a religious ceremony

shape-shifting describes a person who can change into a different shape, animal, or form

spirit the force within a person that is believed to give the body life, energy, and power

suicide the act of killing oneself

supernatural a force for which there is no scientific explanation

traumatic very upsetting, painful, or disturbing

UFOs Unidentified Flying Objects, such as alien spacecraft

yellow fever a serious infection spread by certain mosquitoes

FIND OUT MORE

Books

Beer, Julie. *Weird But True Halloween: 300 Spooky Facts to Scare You Silly.* National Geographic Kids, 2020.

Fitzpatrick, Insha. *Chilling with Ghosts: A Totally Factual Field Guide to the Supernatural.* Quirk Books, 2023.

Hollihan, Kerrie Logan. *Ghosts Unveiled!* (Creepy and True #2). Harry N. Abrams, 2020.

Kelley, K.C. *Lincoln's Ghost* (Haunted History). Bear Claw, 2021.

Williams, Dinah. *Battlefield Ghosts* (True Hauntings #2). Scholastic Nonfiction, 2021.

Websites

Learn about other ghosts of Hampton Court Palace at:
www.hrp.org.uk/hampton-court-palace/history-and-stories/historic-hauntings-at-hampton-court-palace/#gs.1ml6oa

Discover how to hunt ghosts at:
www.ghostsandgravestones.com/how-to-ghost-hunt

Read about more White House ghosts at:
www.whitehousehistory.org/press-room/press-backgrounders/white-house-ghost-stories

Are ghosts real? Read about this idea at:
www.wonderopolis.org/wonder/are-ghosts-real

Publisher's note to educators and parents:
All the websites featured above have been carefully reviewed to ensure that they are suitable for students. However, many websites change often, and we cannot guarantee that a site's future contents will continue to meet our high standards of educational value. Please be advised that students should be closely monitored whenever they access the Internet.

INDEX

About the Author

Louise Spilsbury is an award-winning children's book author. She has written countless books about history and science. In writing and researching this book, she is more spooked than ever by the idea of ghosts and haunted places!